THIS BOOK BELONGS TO:

_____

To Dahlia Chery Bastien, you have inspired us to do and be so much more. Never stop being curious.

-Mom & Dad

DAHLIA & FRIENDS

all the toys in the world

www.dahliaandfriends.com

Copyright © 2021 Jacques Bastien and Dahcia Lyons-Bastien.

All rights reserved. This book or parts thereof may not be reproduced in any form, stored in any retrieval system, or transmitted in any form by any means—electronic, mechanical, photocopy, recording, or otherwise—without prior written permission of the publisher, except as provided by United States of America copyright law. For permission requests, write to the publisher, at the address below.

ISBN: 978-1-9547-3900-0 (Paperback)
ISBN: 978-1-9547-3901-7 (Hardcover)
ISBN: 978-1-9547-3902-4 (EPub)

Library of Congress Control Number: 2021931118

Any references to historical events, real people, or real places are used fictitiously. Names, characters, and places are products of the author's imagination.

Illustration by Wendi Hendra Saputra.

Printed and published in the United States of America. First printing edition 2021.

SHADE Books, imprint of SHADE MGMT, LLC
1732 1st Ave #20377, New York NY 10128

www.shadebooks.co

DAHLIA & FRIENDS

all the toys in the world

written by
JACQUES BASTIEN
and **DAHCIA LYONS-BASTIEN**

illustrated by
WENDI HENDRA SAPUTRA

SHADE BOOKS

So many toys, so many toys!
They're all that I think about, want, and enjoy.

It could be a doll, a truck, or a kite,
I think about toys every day and every night.

My name is Dahlia and here is my tale
of an idea I had that can't possibly fail.

One day while outside under a full sky of blue,
I had an idea too good to be true.

What if I could play with all the toys in the world,
from everyone I know... every boy and every girl?

I'd come up with a deal where we trade for the day.
"My toys for yours? Now, what do you say?"

This way we all get a chance to see how
Mason's race car works and play with Noëlle's cow.

Jubilee has always wanted a scooter to try
and Kaden wants blocks to stack to the sky.

Playing with the same toys can be boring, it's true.
Now, you can have new toys anytime you want to.

And we'd all work together, one big happy team.
So many toys, like a wonderful dream.

Every day is like your birthday, as we trade and we play.
And the best part for parents, there's no need to pay.

As a team we'll make sure everyone gets a turn.
We will share, we will play, we will grow, we will learn.

We'll all need to be patient and so careful too.
We don't want broken toys, that's the right thing to do.

Maleya and Leighla will trade for the day,
and if they want, work out a more permanent stay.

This idea will catch on and sweep across the nation,
From New York to Florida... to any destination.

Every town in the country, every city on earth,
Paige's bunny might make it all the way to Perth.

It's time to share this idea with my team,
because I'll need their help to realize this dream.

So after a talk with the crew before dinner,
the decision was made, my idea is a **WINNER**!

So that is the tale of how me and my friends
thought through an idea, from beginning to end.

If you have an idea that will make the world better,
share it with your friends, and build it together.

THE END

Dahlia's Friends
(characters in order of appearance)

Dahlia	Jubilee
Leah	Mom
Ezra	Dad
Jayden	Maleya
Mason	Leighla
Noëlle	Paige
Kaden	Namar

View more friends at
www.dahliaandfriends.com

CPSIA information can be obtained
at www.ICGtesting.com
Printed in the USA
BVHW020020260122
627124BV00002B/44